Dancing
Dancing in slippers
On a hard wood floor
I'm just dancing away
Nothing I want anymore

I want to get away
Get away from the black
Maybe get away from the grey
I'm just covering up the white

The semantics, the definitions
The lies, the truth, right in between
Sick of being the spectator
In front of your eyes I go unseen

DEVIANCE
WITHOUT BOUNDS

SCREAMS
MUFFLED SOUNDS
TORTURE
MINOR PAIN
DOMINANCE
SALTY RAIN
PLEASURE
A DARK WAY
SATISFACTION
PRICE TO PAY

Do the clouds move?
Or is it the sun?

It should be obvious
Everything is one

The moon hides
And it glows
The seas answer
The sun, it knows

Pink horizons
A rainbow hue
Perfect timing
It's all so new

Tell Sue
I said Hi

Then I
Committed
Suicide
A firefly
Extinguished
By the rain

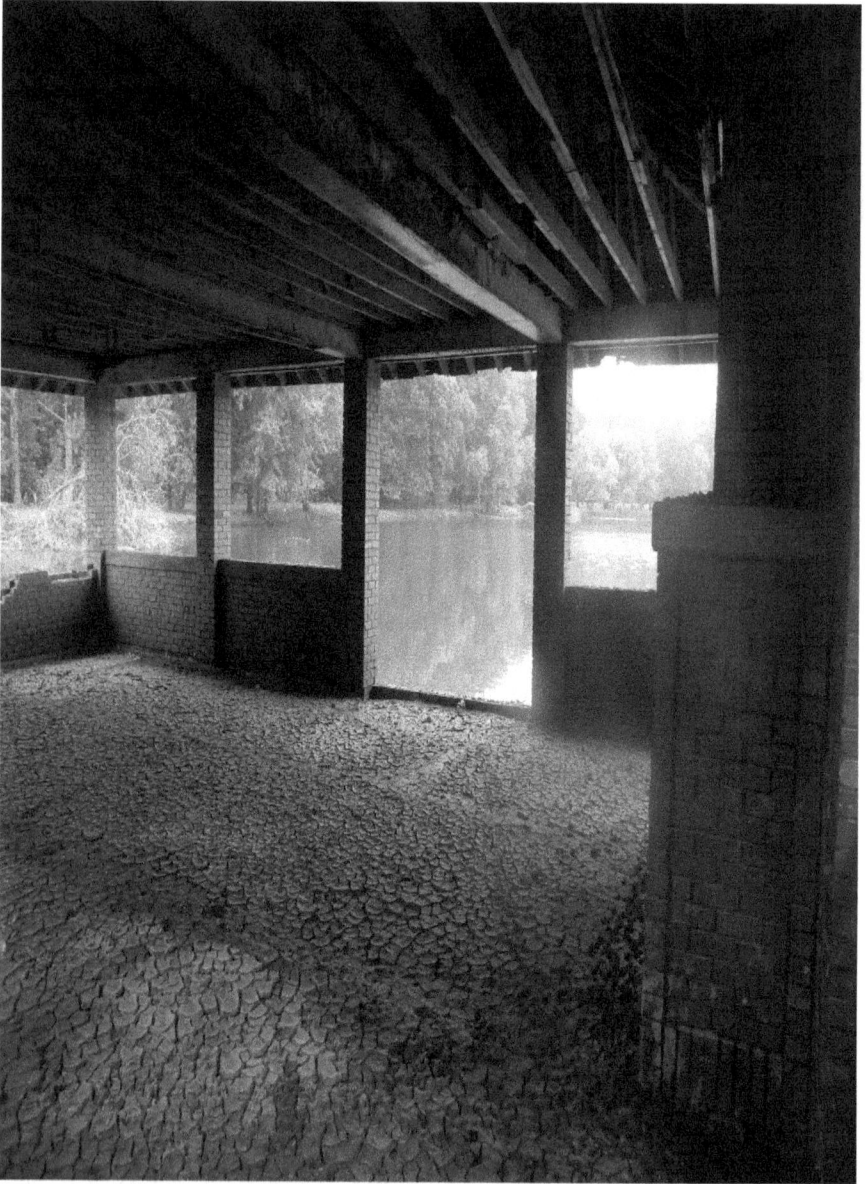

I won't play games on my phone
As just to pass the time away
No more sitcoms, no reality shows
Wasting it all is such a crime

You deserve the pleasure you get
If you folly in mundane things
I don't want to be numb anymore
I'll step up to what the world brings

I want to feel the blood in my veins
I don't want to sleep my life away
I want a blade held to my throat
I don't want to keep the sharks at bay

Let me just peruse your bad ink
So I know what it is you stand for
I'll find my way into seclusion
I don't want to play your games anymore

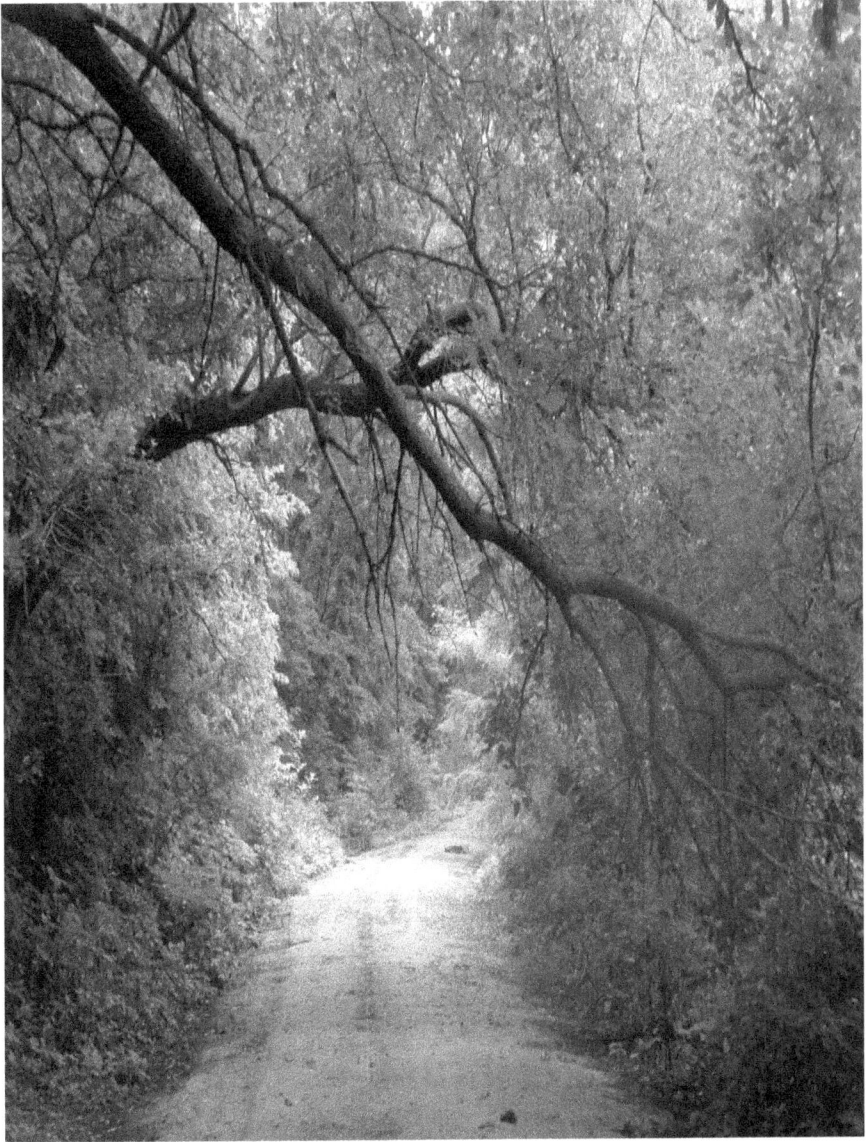

I don't have keys
I have no home
No car, no place to go

The family is gone
The dog is dead

Diabetes has my toe

No hand to hold
No voice to hear
My walls are the sky

Haunted by a face
A scent I still smell
I no longer ask why

Footsteps echo
Are they mine?
A burnt sun sets

Clock hands freeze
No past, no future
Casino's not taking bets

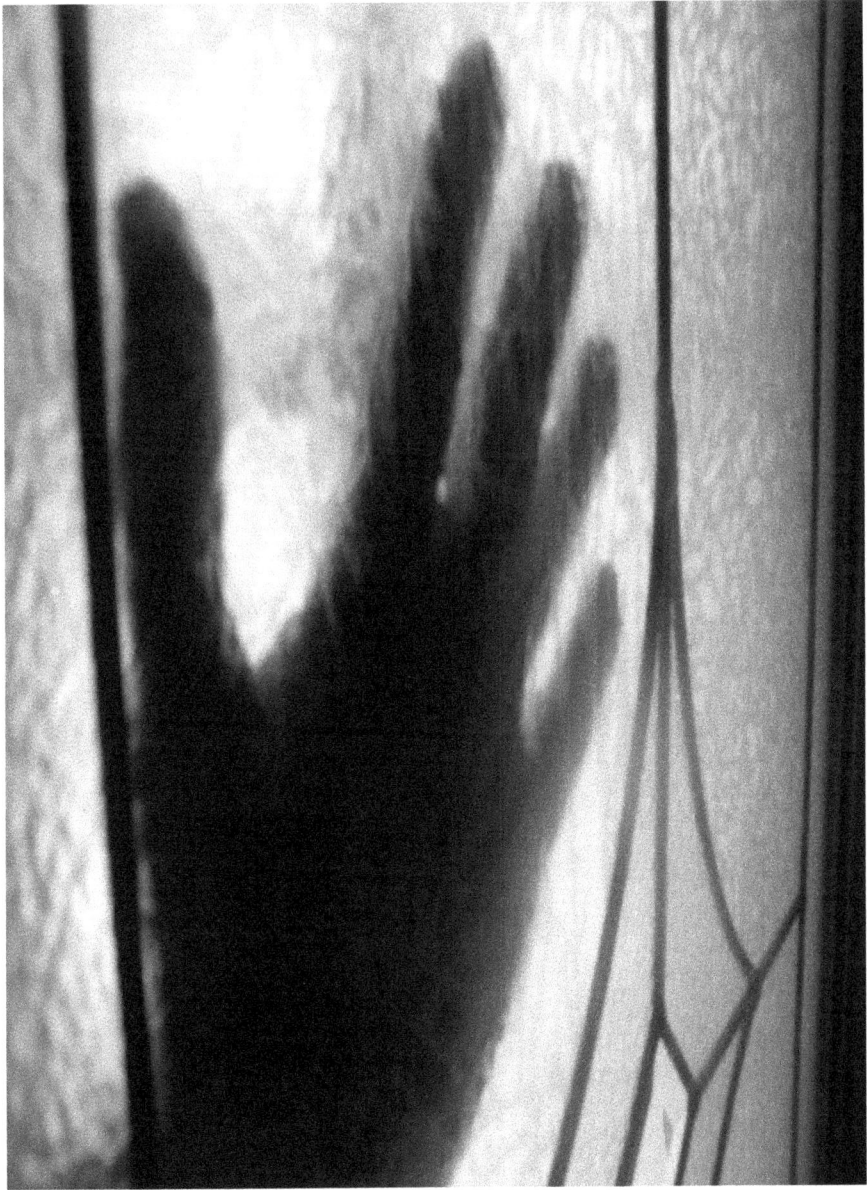

I miss Colorado
I miss my old life
I miss my kid Alexis
I really miss Julie my wife

I miss having my art on the wall
I miss seeing my books on a shelf
I miss the pit bull "King"
I miss being my old self

I miss going to the Draft
I miss talking while having beers
I miss feeling at peace
I miss those seven years

I miss fucking you
I miss what seems real
I miss orange sunsets
I miss a good Mexican meal

I don't miss the hospital'
I don't miss watching you die
I don't miss seeing you bald
I don't miss refusing to cry

I miss all my liquor stores
I miss not knowing the story
I miss not feeling helpless
I miss feeling like Cory

Kindergarten Friend
Painting
Childhood
Friend

Kindergarten'
Later
Black
Ice
No
Seatbelt
He
Told
Me
He
Felt
Cold
Darkness

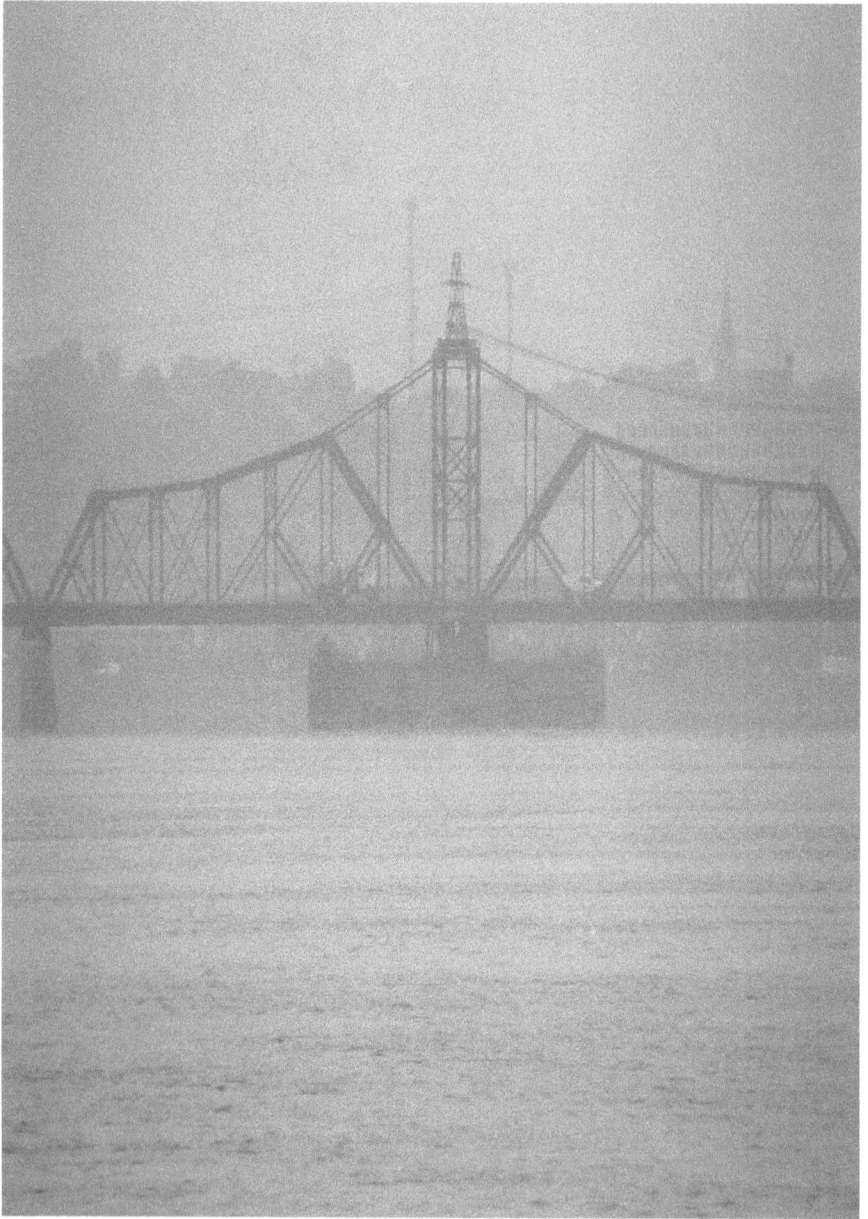

Not Afraid

The focal point of the day
Is when I can open that first beer
That has been the story of my life
Day in, day out, year after year

There were never any obstacles

Just alternative times to be figured out
I can be sober if I must a while longer
I just want to be me without the doubt

Day or night are such arbitrary rules
Great are the days when the clock doesn't tick
The joy of living in a sunless cell
Whiskey in my coffee after I called off sick

You know that your God is smiling on you
On those rare occasions you get to do the process twice
A nice little nap after the morning round
I offer up my night as the next sacrifice

I drink one last shot to you my old friends
What a great pair of lovers we have always made
I never thought I would let go of my sweet lady
This time will be the last
Because for the first time
I am not afraid

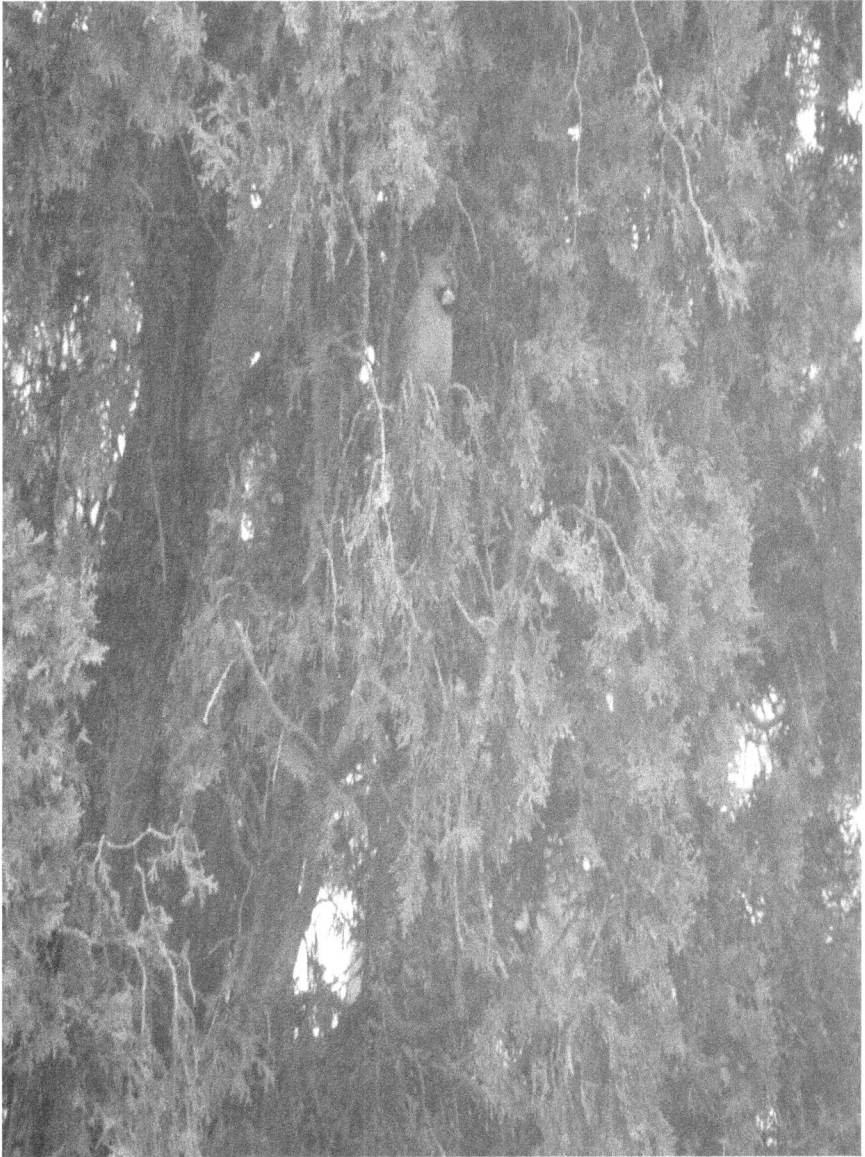

Out of balance
A jigsaw life
Have no faith
Dull rusty knife

Walls to the sky

A big dark maze
Darting wide eyes
A thick grey haze

Strange silence
Lost in sight
Invisible aura
No moon at night

Nowhere to rise
No more hellos
No more goodbyes

One last try
Attempt to sync
I can do this
Just need a drink

Snowflakes
The snowflakes here look
Like floating diamonds

The wind doesn't
Drive them into
Your face
They just seem
To enjoy the trip down
Like ice cubes
In a parachute
But so much more
Delicate
And
Blissful to
What might be
The demise
Or the snowflakes
Become
This summers
fireflies

STEP UP YOUR GAME

I got to the valley last night
But the airport wasn't there
It was just my old self
Giving my new self a stare

I looked into the old eyes
All I could see was shame
An insignificant voice from the sky
Nonchalantly said, "Step up your game"

The old self laughed and took pity
He knew what the new one had been
through
"You've been living in the past for too
long.
Don't you think it's time to find
something new?"

All at once, I was just alone in the valley
It felt I was standing atop a million
graves
As much as I love the mountains and
prairies
It's time to sit on the sand and watch
the waves

Things are starting to make sense to me
I think the fog I'm in has lasted too long
It's time for me to start dancing again
I have to do it, quit waiting for the
right song

Sullen river
Dreams below
No longer young
Ebb and flow

Visions then
Reality now
No appointment
Here somehow

Trail of crumbs
Can't get back
Who was that?
I'm you Jack

Can't relax
Going away
Stop stop stop
Hear what I say

Time warps
Intersections
Predestinations
Insurrections

Sidetracks
Harrowing cries
Lit cigarettes
Sweet goodbyes

Hollow words
Months and years
Crowded loneliness
Silent tears

A reunion
There you are
Always there
A distant star

I watched you walk up the stairs
You said your favorite show was on
It was something about a fairy tale
You moved so gracefully 'til you were gone

There is no sound coming from the room

I have faith that you are in there
You keep saying that nothing has changed
I hope you know that I really care

I loved to watch you sleep
I tell myself that this is nothing at all
Just a blip in the scheme of things
You're as close as a long distance call

There was a time I thought it was over
You shook your head and looked away
The room turned cool and dark
I knew you had nothing left to say

Now here you are back again
A comfortable silence is all we feel
Our souls are once again together
The bloody wounds begin to heal

VERSE

This is me
Writing some verse
I don' t know why
I didn' t rehearse

This is a poem
I don't know what it is about
I just have a paper and pen
Feels like my soul needs out

Am I going into the future?
Maybe I'll rethink the past
This doesn't mean anything
How long will it last?

Okay, I'll finish it now
Poetry can be ridiculous art
As can anything else
Olfactory art by a fart

YOUNGSTERS

I love listening to you younger guys
It seems like you have it all figured out

I remember your excitement, I thought I did too
I'm becoming an old man, and I still don't know what it's about

You stumble through your twenties and thirties
You hope that out of the blue the right one comes along
You've been through the sluts, and the heartbreakers
You lay awake at night and wonder what went wrong

Then one night you're sitting in bar minding your own business
You have another beer while you're waiting out the rain
You might think about the situations that you let pass you by
You sit next to a girl and realize that you share a common pain

That girl is like nobody you have ever met before
After a few minutes of talking to her, you know that she will change
your life
Three hours after you meet, you are having wild, passionate sex
The thought crosses your mind, "Is this my next wife?"

You just don't know what you're getting into when you're young
This isn't a girl you just fuck, this is a soul mate
I implore you not to get trapped by the games of youth
Life comes at you either way too early or way too late

www.ingramcontent.com/pod-product-compliance
Lightning Source LLC
Chambersburg PA
CBHW060618030426
42337CB00018B/3116